The Price of the Repair

poems by

Jennifer Bisbing

Finishing Line Press
Georgetown, Kentucky

The Price of the Repair

Publisher: Leah Huete de Maines
Editor: Christen Kincaid
Cover Art: Scott W. Parker
Author Photo: Larry Chait
Cover Design: Emma Bilyk

Order online: www.finishinglinepress.com
also available on amazon.com

Author inquiries and mail orders:
Finishing Line Press
PO Box 1626
Georgetown, Kentucky 40324
USA

Contents

For the ancient rocks that let me climb on their backs

I Hope They Never Pave My Road

That cloud of grit tailing me is the only
reliable evidence of my escape

Last Winter Raged Past

I sit toes tucked in waterproof shoes
inches from the crooked shore
Afraid to let the wet in
Spring seems fickle today,
hard to trust a sun
lost in clouds
I came fishing
but not for something scaly
something slippery
though I'm unwilling
to get in a boat
I sit until the cold of winter creeps back in
The cold of being gutless
The cold of losing my voice

Whispering Pollen

A code of clicks, collective swooshes
Louder, then a faint tap of two wheat seeds
These slender stems don't
stop when the breeze ceases
They hold on
to the momentum of what they need to say

A Tree on Top of the Moon

You peek up from that low valley,
fall slowly down the other side
of the mountain

Here on rocks of lava,
I see no water,
I only see you
and a long way down

Wind, will you stay with me?
But no, wind never sticks around
I have these roots, this trunk,
I am planted on top of the moon

Find me water
Blow in the clouds
Wait, gently
Have you seen those broken limbs,
leftover gnarled parts?
I want to stay whole

I cling
on top of the moon
The cliff so close
If I lean too far,
will you catch me
like you do the birds?

Coffee (and who)

Blackness
drenches every corner
until the moon
leers in my bedroom
I slumber in its spotlight
'til the owl wakes me
I open the door
wrapped in
wings of blankets
We both wait
You don't move a feather
Until a distant
"who"
followed by a louder
"who"
Then you drum
the air with
your wings
and pass
through the moonlight

Under
your nocturnal spell
I retreat inside
make black coffee
Each bitter sip
reminds me of who
preys on my mind

The Lookout

Echoes of a chainsaw pierce the fire lookout
It's whirling hum, screaming, cutting the hush
Turns out—the droning motor—merely water
boiling on the wood burning stove—hissing out the splitting seams
I want the screeching to be somewhere distant
Not inside, not so close

Pure Gold

The miners stripped this high desert
of most things precious
But show me the last vein in this
hot valley
Separate me from the dirt
Show me where
the gleaming thread leads
Let me descend through
this unfarmable land,
with the Holy Grail
in my callused hands

The Missions

Why didn't you pay the fee?
The box just wanted five and the land could use more

You stealing again?

Did the ranch hand leave the barn light on
or are you in there now

building your escape plan?

What do you hope to find
out past the highway signs?

A glimpse of the whistling woman
A golden eagle's yellow shoes

The Writing on the Diner's Bathroom Wall

[Blacked out name] I don't know why
you do anything you do
                    I just know my taste buds have dulled
for what you put on my plate

Collecting Rocks

At 9,000 feet, switchbacks, the only markers of distance
                As my feet traverse the unworn trail,
where roots and rocks claim it back, I see no one, hear
only what wants to be heard   The magpie's
warning, the squeak of a mountain squirrel   I
lose all definitions of home, planted only in movement
            Over the ridge, the fir forest opens,
welcoming me at the exact moment I think of turning
back   Walking on, even as my feet grow unsure,
        I step around the trail-closed sign
      The ground crumbles below my boot   Soil
waterfalls with me, down, quickly, toward where I
started   Grasping at roots, anything to stall gravity
        After thirty feet, a rock places itself below
my boots   I land somewhere between the sky
and the riverbed   —A strange place again—
        Another I must climb out of

Next Rest Stop, Hole-in-the-Wall

Oil Creek leaked hate all through this place
Not even a stray 100-year-old Cottonwood
where the creek dried up
could protect me
from sizzling heat
A rattlesnake joins me in the shade
Not until
I darted through the oil fields of Wyoming did I fear
what was coming next, up the road
—the rotting town of Little America—
The tycoon took the dream, left nothing behind
And died with three billion sitting in the bank

Devouring Distance

Wildness grows in me
one like I envision a cowboy
has under a hat

Finding a hole
in the fence,
I joined the feral cattle
and roamed far
from the branding iron

Men with Guns Afraid of Grasshoppers

I find refuge
in a thousand blades,
the uncut grass slants toward
the earth in prayer for rain
Resting on top
of the hill, I pluck
flat, green strands
out of the dry dirt
Gently tugging
each one, wondering
can I pull out the root?
With slim success, and all
this summer's daylight,
I keep pulling, gingerly

Down the hill
stands my family's run-down,
two-story farmhouse
It lightly sways,
begs for a fresh
coat of paint
A patch of pines,
stand straight
like soldiers, attempting
to keep out wind, the intruder

I hold my grandad's old Colt
shoot at dilapidated farm equipment
that litters the unkept land I inherited
his fortress surrounded by a trench
Dug to keep
the war from
following him home

Act Two

I've started to yell from the ridgetops
But say very little at dinner

Stalled on 20 East

Jumping the barbed wire fence
I land in brown, matted grass
Wondering who
curled up under this big sky,
slept in this rotting life
Somewhere between two fenced off farms—I stand still
Surrounded by wild rye,
I frame a frame,
marking my moment in time with one small push,
freezing it
until it's lost in my pile of stuff
Lost like the rusting junk on this
abandoned high-desert homestead
The farmer once pushed patches of dirt
to make it richer,
to feed a hunger
that only hard, dry bread leaves
Did the lack of gold in the hills,
cause him to lie down in weeds and starve his horse?
Parched,
perhaps the snow tempted him north
Or the truck's gears gave out
Now it poses for a shot,
pleading to move
Paint shads pulled free by the dry wind
Bash against my skin
Did this splintered schoolhouse double as a church?
Dead bolted from the outside
is this where the children learned that the best answer is maybe
and not to ask why?
I stop asking as well, click off
another frozen instant in this ever-changing weather

God's country abandoned,
My camera steals what's left

Goldie's Diner in Neon (minus a burned-out e)

The waitress looks hard
like she should be throwing down whiskey
instead of watered-down coffee in brown mugs
The checkered floor looks shabby
from Karl's spur marks, perhaps?
Probably just from the same folks' tired feet,
walking the same way up to the counter,
year after year staying the course
directly to Peggy, who bakes all the pies
Apples laced with sugar waft through
when the front door swings open

At the closest table—ladies whisper
local gossip or something about the city girl
who just sat down alone in the tattered vinyl booth,
minding her out of town business over eggs and toast

Love sits across the Formica tabletop,
but the seat is empty
If he was there, he'd be
wearing his worn-out overalls,
the ones I was always trying to replace
the ones I buried him in
I order his favorite pie
and only take a fork-full
He used to protest when I stole a bite
Leaving here
means I leave him

Diner Counter (point of view)

The cleaver raises up
Slices through the chicken breast bone
I am two pieces now
The half left when I gave up everything for you
lies listless in this plucked skin
The other half yearns for
wholeness—impossible since the blade slid thru
And what will the cook do
with that piece that thumps and flutters

Boat Sinking in His Lawn

The trackwork just ends—straggly weeds hiding cut iron
How did he decide we didn't need
to go any further? How did he settle on
drilling stakes into the earth
anchored to this nowhere?
Leaving those following his straight line, stranded

Fog Swallowed the Valley

The air stalled in this
frontier town
Its heart stuck in an old groove
under the crumbling paving bricks
A gunman robbed this valley
of its wildness,
slashing it into subdivisions
I sit uninvited on his front stoop

The local rodeo
still lives for those eight seconds
New cowboys, new horses
from ranches down the county road,
one occasionally ripped
out of the wild across the state line
I pay the admission fee

Generations settled in plots
where the gunman told them to stay
I won't buy this man's stolen land

The Horse Whisperer

Every rescued horse saunters across the corral to his
brassy bull-legged stride   But he never
whispers   Everything he does is loud
         His four-wheeler howls, gurgles, spits, a
rougher ride than an unbroken horse   His
lawn mower clanks, roars, slaughtering an army of grass
         He power-washes the house and "nearly
all" dirty surfaces, blasting every molecule of silence
         He never stops talking at a volume that
would curdle the milk in a librarian's cup of tea
         though he never turns away a homeless horse
         They overflow from one field to the
next—his sea of manes in the high desert

Up Switchbacks

After dodging ruts in the road, deep past the swimming
hole and children chattering   An altitude where breath is
threadbare and modern civilization a memory
       Wings bat stillness, sounding like horse hooves
approaching   Where trees wear the most
fashionable, flowing skirts   Smooth skin boring
in the presence of ponderosa grooves   Pale
compared to the yellow-breasted bird   And
the berries making everyone drunk   How easy it
is to stumble and forget the way back

Uncommon Places (in common)

She fed the fillies
filled the llama's bucket
patched up the barn cat's broken tail
all before she told me she was
constantly getting in trouble
She walks away, only after she spit
her whole life out on the front stoop
her best years behind her, following like a long shadow
her limp and gait match the horse sent out to pasture

her son wants to shoot them both

Soiled Hands

What was harsh in him was pushed down
under the shoveled walkway
Hidden in the handpicked cherries and
homemade soup

He built the windowless shed,
not for my garden tools,
but for him, figuring he'd be kicked out of the house

Our frozen pond is thin this year
I crack it with a pitchfork

Along our bluff—steel rolls over steel,
slapping silence
I remember now
where he buried his rage
The factory
The mine
The mill

I dig in the stripped soil
with his worn-out gloves
Planting what will not grow

The Price of the Repair

I watch the handyman fiddle with something that wasn't
broken
Until he breaks it

Now we can't look one another in the eye

The songbird chirps, tweets at the frequency of a bomb's
countdown

Why don't people have hazard lights?
Just a flip of a switch—alert others
to slow down

The handyman digs deeper—
I didn't see it coming
The muck explodes

No Vacancy

Turning the key
A large bloodstain in the carpet greets me
I paid
for a bed just to sleep off the drive
Instead I stumble onto an old crime scene
Too tired to change rooms
all I can do is think about you
why you had to die here—in this drive-thru town
where people haven't come up with a good reason to stay
You didn't have a choice
You didn't make it out of this room,
your last view
this god-awful patterned bedspread

A Truck on My Tail

His tires touch the yellow line,
making me uneasy
Then he's gone, and I can't
imagine where except into the river

Which bend did he lose control?

Strangers should stop
following me
I've memorized this road
each curve, each bump, every dip
where the cliff juts out, where to tap the brake
before the blind curve, where you need
to cross the yellow line to make the turn at double the posted speed

I won't slow down for their mistakes

While eyeing Butte's pit, a semi's gust shakes something loose
All that I've been lugging, unhitches, slides across traffic, over the
rumble strip
I won't slow down
Someone else will be happy with my left-behind life

John T. "Jack" Gilmer's Misspelled Town

Your hotel hasn't had a guest
since 1929, but through the fire-scorched trees,
I hear chattering voices of men returning from the mine

Slop spills over the soles of my shoes
My steps are labored, this ghost town pulls me down
Trying to keep me stuck in the past

Who buys a plot in this shifting sludge?
Fool's genes, to think this lead-filled land will bring them new
fortune
The gold is in Sun Valley, locked behind gated houses
And slippery deals

I run before I get stuck in someone else's mess

In a twin town on the other side of the Plains
My great grandfather opened a hardware store
I believe in tools, wrenches, nailing into something solid

Triumph (unincorporated community)

Idaho, you keep
bucking me
like a proud
bull.

Your grit is under
my nails.

Your unmuffled, wide-mirrored pickups
roar around me.

Your mountains took my strength.
Though
there is a place in me
that you can't soil
with your grimy games.

I'm buckled in
leaving you,
your rattlesnakes and arsenic water.

Release the Hammer, Put Down the Weapon

A million ways to be a woman in this world
and I choose to walk with trees
I toss out my phone at the rest stop
Jump back on 90
Take the next exit, next grassy two track
toward an unmarked trail
bury my burdens under the larch, the one that turns late
partner with mud, walk together, up
up, until we crest, boots pointed down
to the other side of the canyon cut
by its battle with change
One long look over the vista to Paradise Valley
One long look back to where we met
This is where we go beyond the finish line
Beyond anyone else's markers

ACKNOWLEDGMENTS

A warm-hearted thank you to the editors of the publications in which some of these poems have appeared, sometimes in different forms:

Whiskey Tit Journal, "The Price of the Repair"
Typehouse Literary Magazine, "Goldie's Diner in Neon (minus a burned-out e)," "The Writing on the Diner's Bathroom Wall." "Diner Counter (point of view)"
CIRQUE Journal, "The Missions"

Thanks to my family, dear friends, teachers, and editors for your insight and encouragement. And thank you, Scott W. Parker for the use of your art for the cover.

Jennifer Bisbing is aan award-winning book editor and photographer originally from the Midwest who now lives on Whidbey Island. Raised by a renowned forensic scientist, Bisbing's murder mystery *Under the Pines* reveals childhood memories of trips to the crime lab. With family dinner conversations notoriously leading to murder cases, it's no surprise her poetry has a few lingering villains. She writes book reviews for *Montana Quarterly*, edits for several national and international publishers, and can be found online at *jenniferbisbing.com*.

www.ingramcontent.com/pod-product-compliance
Lightning Source LLC
Chambersburg PA
CBHW022054080426
42734CB00009B/1339